D1712453

Professional Portfolios for Practicing Teachers

by
Ann Adams Bullock
and
Parmalee P. Hawk

ISBN 0-87367-683-1
Copyright © 2001 by the Phi Delta Kappa Educational Foundation
Bloomington, Indiana

Table of Contents

Introduction

Portfolios have become important in all stages of the teaching profession: preservice, induction, and inservice. They are used for self-assessment, awards, and evaluations. Some teachers create them for teacher of the year awards, while others document their professional growth for evaluation purposes or to apply for National Board Certification. Portfolios also are used by both preservice and inservice teachers to document their professional development, to measure preservice teacher knowledge, or for certification.

There are many benefits to developing portfolios. The major benefit of developing a portfolio is that it gives teachers control over their own professional growth. Portfolios also allow teachers to document for supervisors multiple accomplishments throughout the year. They allow teachers to set professional goals and to change their classroom practices based on the reflection inherent in developing a portfolio.

This fastback provides information about the basic principles of portfolio development. The types of portfolios, with examples and reflections, are outlined.

Types of Portfolios

A portfolio is not merely a manila file filled with assignments or work, nor is it a scrapbook of memorabilia. A portfolio is an organized, goal-driven collection of documents (Campbell et al. 1997). For a teacher, a portfolio is a collection that tells a story.

There are three types of portfolios: process, product, and showcase. Each type is compiled for a different audience. However, each also has four basic components:

1. *They have a specific purpose.* Portfolios are done for a specific reason (for example, awards, evaluation, or licensure).
2. *They are developed for a specific audience.* Someone will review the portfolio when it is completed.
3. *They contain work samples, commonly called 'evidence.'* Evidence is the "stuff" or "things" that are put into the portfolio. The teacher's evidence should include lesson plans, units of study, and other professional documents.
4. *They have reflections.* These are written thoughts on the evidence contained in the portfolio.

The Process Portfolio

The purpose of a process portfolio is to evaluate a person's progress in one or more areas over a given period of time. This type of portfolio commonly is used in teacher evaluation, where professional goals provide the foundation for choosing evidence.

Suppose a teacher had the professional goal of using a greater variety of strategies in the classroom. The process portfolio would show how various strategies were used to improve student participation, comprehension, and success. The developer would choose evidence to show how a variety of strategies were used and how students progressed over time. Reflections would focus on those strategies and their impact on students. For example, the teacher might describe a lesson focusing on using cooperative groups then note the successes and the areas that need improvement when the strategy is used again.

The evidence in a process portfolio should represent both successes and weaknesses so that a clear portrayal of the teacher's progress is given.

The Product Portfolio

A product portfolio is similar to a process portfolio except that it is meant to be one of a number of portfolios judged by someone else. These portfolios have specific, required evidence so that those who compiled them can be compared consistently against common criteria. Teachers might create a product portfolio to show how a school goal is being met, to seek a license, or to compete for an award.

For example, in a district that set a goal that each teacher would use authentic assessments, the portfolios would contain evidence to show how a teacher creates and implements such assessments. Each portfolio might contain staff development information, sample student assessments with grading criteria, and teachers' reactions to using authentic assessments. Reflections would include descriptions of how authentic assessments were included in the classroom, their strengths, and areas that need improvement. In this example, the principal might assess the portfolios from each teacher in the school.

Often, national standards are used as the criteria for product portfolios. This type of portfolio is used in the National Board process when teachers meet specific standards and tell how they do so. Product portfolios also are used in some states (for example, North Carolina) by beginning teachers who must do specific activities to show they meet the specific standards.

The Showcase Portfolio

A showcase portfolio is developed by a teacher to serve as a collection of the teacher's best work. Showcase portfolios often are used for job interviews or awards. The distinguishing characteristic of a showcase portfolio is that it is completely individualized and is based on the perceptions of the developer about himself or herself.

Organizing a Portfolio

The first consideration when developing a portfolio is how to organize it. Common methods include sorting the evidence by sections, goals, standards, or domains. The purpose of the portfolio often will determine how it is organized.

However the portfolio is organized, it should include a table of contents and a title page. This is necessary if the portfolio is to be read by someone other than the person who compiled it. The portfolio also should be organized so that each section is clearly delineated. This can be done by using tab dividers for each section. Another option is to use a different color paper for each section or to used colored paper to identify when sections begin.

The portfolio also should include an introductory section that includes a brief explanation of how the portfolio is organized. Many teachers also add a résumé and a statement about their philosophy of education in the introductory section.

Many teachers use plastic page protectors to hold the evidence so their work is not damaged. This is important if the portfolio will be reviewed by many people.

In addition, evidence on large sheets of paper can be folded and slipped into a page protector so that it fits in the portfolio.

Clip art and other graphics are optional for the portfolio. The depth of evidence and reflection should be more important than the aesthetics. However, a sloppy product with multiple spelling errors is not acceptable from any professional.

Finally, the developer must decide how to package the portfolio. Three-ring binders are the most common container. For a professional look, the binder should be black or white. If possible, use a binder that has a plastic sleeve on the outside of its cover. This allows the teacher to insert a label, thus further identifying the portfolio.

Depending on the purpose and nature of the portfolio, other ways to package it may be more appropriate. For example, the materials included may be so bulky that a binder will not hold them. In those cases, an expandable folder or even a plastic file box with a handle might be more appropriate.

The Importance
of Reflection

Without written reflections, a portfolio is just a scrapbook. The reflection gives substance to the collection and guides the reader. Reflection requires the teacher to think about what they are doing, why they are doing it, what the outcomes are, and how the information can be used for continuous improvement (McLaughlin and Vogt 1998). It is reflection that allows any individual to improve and grow.

The emphasis on teacher reflection grows out of a body of literature that emerged during the 1980s that describes the need for, approaches to, and benefits of reflection (Cady 1998, Sparks-Langer and Colton 1991). As educators engage in instruction and then reflect on it, the process offers insights into various dimensions of the teaching and learning process that can lead to better teaching (Schon 1987). If professionals never reflect on their actions or beliefs, improvement will be minimal or nonexistent.

Defining Reflection

Reflection is the process of looking at information or events, thinking about and analyzing them, and then using the results to change or enhance future events. Teachers should consistently reflect on their own practice and on the achievement of their students.

Teaching reflections consist of three vital components: description, analysis, and planning (Bullock and Hawk 2000).

The description is an important segment for the audience of the portfolio. It should emphasize who, what, when, where, and how and should provide the foundation for the rest of the reflection. If a clear description is provided, the other two components of the reflection will be easier to write.

Following is a sample description from a sixth-grade teacher.

> This piece of evidence is a social studies lesson on map skills taught to a sixth-grade class with a diverse population of students with varied learning abilities. Things considered when planning this lesson were 1) the prior knowledge of the students, and 2) that this class has children who become disengaged easily. As a result of these factors, I filled my lesson with various activities that required participation. When planning this lesson, I developed pictures and models for students so they would understand the concept I was teaching.
>
> When teaching this lesson, I took on the role of a coach. I gave instruction and then allowed students time to do activities. I informally assessed students during the activities. I looked at students' body language, facial expression, interest, effort, and ability to get the "right" answer. If they seemed to have an interest, positive body language, and an ability to get the "right" answer, I would move on in the lesson. However, if they failed to possess

these things, I would reteach, review, or give another example on which they could work. This choice was based on the signals I received from the students.

This social studies lesson addressed the state curriculum goal, "demonstrate an understanding of reading and analyzing maps." I did this by instructing students how to use the map key to determine places and things on the map. In the lesson, I used a variety of maps (topographical, road maps, maps in their books, globe) to allow students to see a wide representation of maps in their world. I began by showing a map of our school with a key to it and asked students to find various places using the key. Next, we had a class discussion about our map's key. I grouped students in pairs and had them view a series of other maps. Using an overhead projector, I asked students specific questions about each map. Finally, pairs of students created their own map and key and created five questions about it. They gave their map and questions to another pair of students to answer. At the end of class, I reviewed the vocabulary related to maps.

Next, the teacher must analyze the evidence. Analysis means to break the whole apart and look for patterns. Patterns can include such things as strengths and areas that need improvement. For example, if the evidence was a lesson plan, the teacher would outline the positive components of the plan and its implementation and then emphasize areas to change in the next lesson plan. Teachers who write thoughtful reflections are honest about their own strengths and weaknesses.

Some evidence, such as a workshop certificate, does not require teachers to reflect on how they would improve it.

Following is a sample analysis.

The lesson was successful because students' participated. Also, as judged by informal assessment, students seemed to understand the content of the lesson. However, the lesson was not a complete success, because not every pair could create their own map and key.

Thus I apparently missed certain skills when I taught the lesson. I seemed to dwell on drilling the students on concepts they already understood, which took away from quality instruction time. I also need to use more informal assessments in order to identify students who are having difficulty with maps.

Planning is the final stage of reflection, and it is the most important. In this stage, the teachers write about how the evidence has affected them and what implications it has for their future actions.

Teaching this lesson taught me that assessment was necessary and that hands-on activities are enjoyed by my students. Through this teaching experience, I saw firsthand how assessment is essential to good teaching. It is essential because it allows instruction to be centered on what students know and what they need to know. I learned that assessing students within a lesson can help pinpoint the instruction method that works best with the content, environment, and student. In future lessons, I will stop and assess more frequently before moving to the next section or activity.

Second, I found that this class enjoys hands-on activities. Even though three pairs did not do the assignment correctly, everyone enjoyed the kinesthetic activity. I will use hands-on activities with this class in the future as part of the curriculum and as a motivator.

Overall, I was extremely pleased with the lesson plan, the teaching experience, and the outcomes that the lesson brought in both the students' understanding of content and in my own professional understanding.

Things to Consider

There are four areas to consider before writing a reflection: audience, clear writing, voice, and bias. These areas also should be used as a checklist after writing a reflection.

Audience. When writing a reflection, the teacher should be aware of the audience at all times. If the audience is a potential employer, the reflection should be written with principals or other supervisors in mind. Knowing the audience allows the teacher to write purposefully.

Clear Writing. A reflection that is well written will enhance any portfolio. Pay specific attention to grammar and spelling. It is especially important to write clearly because it is a skill that a teacher is expected to have. When writing reflections, record thoughts first and then edit. Appropriate professional language should be used for a written reflection.

Voice. The reflection should be written in first person because it is personal. The use of "I" and "me" are appropriate. When the reflection is read, it should be clear that the developer is expressing his or her thoughts.

Bias. Use politically correct terms for all ethnic groups and sensitive language when talking about children with special needs. It is important for the teacher to present himself or herself as a professional and to not offend any audience member who would read the portfolio.

Bias is often a difficult topic for many people to discuss openly. When reading other people's writing, preconceptions and stereotypes about diversity can interfere. For example, a teacher might give the demographics of his or her classroom (for example, the class had 14 Caucasian students and 13 African-American students). Many readers might see such a list of ethnic percentages as commonplace in today's schools, while other readers might see the list of ethnic percentages as biased because it labels certain groups of children. It is helpful to have someone else review reflections for bias.

Following is a sample reflection that illustrates these four factors.

Description. I taught a science lesson to a group of seventh-grade boys and girls from diverse ethnic backgrounds. Most of the students in this class are struggling, and several are repeating this grade. Many of the students have challenging behaviors.

The lesson focused on simple machines. I began by having the students write a few notes about what they knew about simple machines. Then we brainstormed about things we see every day that might be simple machines. Everyone was involved in the discussion. Next I spent 15 to 20 minutes describing each of the six simple machines and demonstrating with models. The students were able to watch, to reflect, and then to work with the simple machines. We discussed as a large group, worked in small groups that I supervised, and reflected individually about what we wrote, about what we saw, and about what we touched. Using a handout that the class completed together, I encouraged vocabulary building and taking notes. During the time left at the end of class, the students worked on hidden-word puzzles that I created just for this lesson.

Since I have taught this class for several weeks, I was very aware of the importance of keeping the students involved, of keeping the lesson going, and of constantly reinforcing the information in a variety of ways (discussion, hands-on activities, taking notes, games). I wanted the information to be accessible. I gave illustrations of simple machines using things with which the students are familiar. I was pleased when one child made the connection between an inclined plane and ramps for wheelchairs at the hospital where his mother works, and when another made the connection between a pulley and an elevator. All the students were interested in handling the simple machines I brought for the lesson. Some of the definitions and equations took more time than I anticipated, so I had to skip the "independent practice" section of my lesson plan; but I thought it was important to teach how simple machines are a part of our everyday lives.

Analysis. I used the textbook as the lesson's foundation, but I constructed my own teaching props. There was a good deal of interest because of the immediacy of the subject material. The lesson was very successful. My students even were able to reduce some complicated machines in the world around them to simple terms. I showed them that science is useful and that it is valuable because it is useful.

The least effective part of the lesson was the puzzle, because it was not clear enough to be useful as a reinforcement tool. I had to do more explaining than I wanted to. Overall, the class was not quiet during the lesson, but much of the noise was constructive. For the most part, my students all stayed on task. The lesson probably included a little more information than could be mastered efficiently in one lesson. The introduction of the simple machines alone, without definitions and equations, would have been more than enough. But, all in all, the lesson was a positive experience for myself and for my students.

Planning. The lesson showed me the value of making academic information relevant and real (see, feel, touch, hold). This class is very social and active, and this type of lesson lent itself to group interaction and discussion. I was able to use these strategies effectively because I was prepared. Maintaining control of the classroom is easier when students are interested, and it is up to me as a teacher to help them see why they should be interested. It is necessary to acknowledge where they are (their need for social interaction) and to recognize what tools will most efficiently get them to where I want them to be. This lesson reinforced the importance of preparation and appropriate teaching strategies based on the needs of my students and the information I am teaching. (Bullock and Hawk 2000)

Using Portfolios to Evaluate Beginning Teachers

Many states across the U.S. are adopting new methods for granting beginning teachers' licenses. One method that is gaining popularity is the creation of a product portfolio with specific activities that correlate with the Interstate New Teacher Assessment and Support Consortium (INTASC) Standards. These standards identify what beginning teachers should know and be able to do and the attitudes they should display in and out of the classroom.

A standards portfolio for beginning teachers is organized in the same way as the product portfolio because the developer is using a set of standards as the organizational guide.

In this section, the INTASC standards have been chosen because they outline good teaching principles for teachers in any discipline or area. However, any type of standards can be used to develop a portfolio. The standards can be the INTASC standards or standards chosen from any national organization, such as the National Middle School Association or the National Council for Teachers of Mathematics. The majority of teaching organizations have developed standards that can be organized and assessed easily.

The INTASC Standards

In 1987, the Council of Chief State School Officers established a consortium to enhance collaboration among states interested in rethinking teacher assessment for initial licensing, as well as for the preparation and induction into the profession. The result was the Interstate New Teacher Assessment and Support Consortium, or INTASC.

The purpose of the INTASC standards is to assess the knowledge, skills, and abilities of beginning teachers. Because of changes in the curriculum and higher requirements for students, there have been new requirements for teachers entering the profession. The INTASC standards have been adopted in more than 17 states as a consistent measure for teacher licensure and competency (INTASC 1992).

Standard One: Content Pedagogy. The teacher understands the central concepts, tools of inquiry, and structure of the discipline he or she teaches and can create learning experiences that make these aspects of subject matter meaningful to students.

Evidence should show that instruction is consistent with state curriculum guidelines. The teacher should show which external resources are used and should demonstrate how the lessons incorporate the central concepts and tools of inquiry of the discipline. For example, the teacher might include a series of lesson plans that are organized around a central topic, concept, or theme and that show connections between different subjects.

Standard Two: Student Development. The teacher understands how children learn and develop, and he or she can provide learning opportunities that support their intellectual, social, and personal development.

Evidence should show that teachers can assess students' prior knowledge and link lessons to that knowledge. Evidence also should demonstrate how the teacher will integrate the lesson with other disciplines or with real-world experiences. And finally, teachers should demonstrate how they will make the students responsible for their own learning.

For example, the evidence might include the physical items used to explain concepts, such as manipulatives used in mathematics classes. It also might include photos of students engaged in activities or group work. In early childhood programs, the evidence might include a developmental checklist that shows the growth of students against particular criteria.

Standard Three: Diverse Learners. The teacher understands how students differ in their approaches to learning and creates instructional opportunities that are adapted to diverse learners.

The evidence should include differentiated lesson plans that show how assignments and strategies are changed or extended to meet the needs of all learners. An example would be a description of how the teacher set up a variety of learning centers around tables or desks, where students can investigate a particular topic in their own way and at their own pace. The teacher also might include a videotape of student projects or speeches, or even a video of the students participating in class.

Standard Four: Critical Thinking. The teacher understands and uses a variety of instructional strategies to encourage students' development of critical-thinking, problem-solving, and performance skills.

The evidence should include the use of multiple teaching strategies for challenging critical thinking. Examples might be a videotape showing the use of higer-order questions; test data showing how students did before and after a lesson, concept, skill, or unit is taught; or even just a description of how the teacher encourages critical thinking for all students.

Standard Five: Motivation and Management. The teacher encourages an understanding of individual and group motivation and behavior to create a learning environment that encourages positive social interactions, active engagement in learning, and self-motivation.

Evidence should include the procedures and rules for classroom management; methods for adjusting the classroom environment to enhance social relationships and student engagement; and ways students are organized for various types of instruction. The teacher should describe any incentive system that is used, including the ways in which the teacher communicates with parents. Lesson plans and videotapes of cooperative learning activities also should be included.

Standard Six: Communication and Technology. The teacher uses knowledge of effective verbal and nonverbal communication to foster active inquiry, collaboration, and supportive interaction in the classroom.

Teachers need to demonstrate their ability to model effective, culturally sensitive communication and to support their students' abilities to express themselves in a variety of ways. Teachers also need to show that they can use of a variety of media to enrich instruction.

Standard Seven: Planning. The teacher plans instruction based on knowledge of subject matter, students, the community, and curriculum goals.

Evidence should include long-range units and daily lesson plans based on curriculum goals, as well as adjusted plans based on unanticipated problems or learner needs.

Standard Eight: Assessment. The teacher understands and uses formal and informal assessment strategies to evaluate students and to ensure the continuous intellectual, social, and physical development of the learner.

Teachers should demonstrate the use of a variety of assessment strategies. They need to show how they use assessment to adjust instruction and to determine their students' learning needs. And they should show how they help students to assess themselves and to set goals. Among the evidence that should be included are teacher-written tests, standardized tests, and a variety of samples of students' work. Other evidence that might be included are samples of students' own portfolios, as well as records of student and parent conferences.

Standard Nine: Professional Development. The teacher is a reflective practitioner who continually evaluates the effects of his or her actions on others (students, parents, and other educators) and who actively seeks out opportunities to grow professionally.

Evidence should include self-evaluations, records of attendance at professional meetings and workshops, and summaries of articles the teacher has read, especially with descriptions of how the ideas were implemented in the teacher's classroom. Other evidence might be a description of the committees on which the teacher has served and volunteer work done beyond the regular school day.

Standard Ten: School/Community Involvement. The teacher fosters relationships with school colleagues, parents, and agencies in the larger community to support students' learning and well-being.

Teachers should document their participation in school activities, their communications with parents, and consultations with other professionals on behalf of students. Examples of this type of evidence are logs or records of home visits, sample letters to parents, and logs of meetings with other agencies and with parents.

Developing an INTASC Portfolio

An INTASC portfolio is intended to show that beginning teachers have the knowledge, skills, and abilities to teach successfully. The audience is usually the state licensing agency. However, local districts may require beginning teachers to complete this same type of activity, making principals or supervisors the audience.

This portfolio usually is organized by the ten standards, but teacher can combine different standards in central teaching responsibilities (for example, instruction and assessment, classroom management and parent communication, professional development and involvement, and working with special needs students). The teacher's reflections emphasize how the standards are met.

The following sample shows how one state adapted an INTASC Standards organizational design, using five activities during a three-year period.

Introduction: Just as in other professions, it is the responsibility of the person seeking a license to demonstrate that he or she has the requisite knowledge, skills, and attitudes. It is the responsibility of the teacher to demonstrate essential teaching competence using the standards developed by the Interstate New Teacher Assessment and Support Consortium (INTASC).

Activities, Standards and Components

Activity 1: Demonstrating your content knowledge and your ability to teach it. (INTASC Standards: 1, 2, 4, 6, 7, 8.)

Required Components: Coordinated Set of Evidence consisting of:
- Unit plan and goals (labeled clearly)
- 5 contiguous lesson plans (with dates)
- Related student work and assessment/test data
- Analysis of student achievement data
- Video for activity 1
- Video information sheet
- Reflection on entire set of evidence

Activity 2: Examining the school-community link: your role in a learning community (INTASC Standard: 10).

Required Components:
- Professional contribution log
- Parent/guardian communication log
- Parent survey(s), example and summary
- Reflection

Activity 3: Focusing on the classroom climate (INTASC Standard: 5).

Required Components:
- Classroom management plan
- Discipline referral rate
- Video showing classroom management plan
- Reflection

Activity 4: Addressing students' unique learning needs (INTASC Standards: 2,3,5, 8,10).

Required Components:
- Two case studies
- Addressing students' unique learning needs
- Related student work
- Student test/assessment data
- Video for Activity 4
- Video information sheet
- Reflection

Activity 5: Appraising yourself as a professional (INTASC Standard: 9).

Required Components:
- Beginning teacher individualized growth plan
- Self-administered interview (clearly labeled) for three years
- Summative evaluation for three years (North Carolina Department of Public Instruction 2001)

Teaching Portfolios for Inservice Teachers

Principals evaluate teachers throughout the school year. Usually, these evaluations are conducted during announced or unannounced observations, and the principals use some type of approved instrument. After the observation, principals share their beliefs about strengths and weaknesses with the teachers.

The active participant in this process is the principal. The teacher usually listens and responds. This results in the teacher having a passive role in an important part of a process that could enhance his or her development as a teacher.

Portfolios are a positive alternative to traditional teacher evaluation because they allow teachers to grow professionally while showing competence. The audience is the principal or immediate supervisor of the teacher, such as a department chairperson. The opportunity to develop a portfolio as a continuing teacher usually is reserved for the tenured teacher.

Teachers and administrators choose to implement professional portfolios for several reasons:

1. Portfolios are an alternative to traditional forms of assessment, thus allowing teachers more of a voice

in their evaluation. When used in addition to traditional methods, portfolios can be a positive experience because they blend several types of data about teaching.

2. Teachers become more reflective about their practice through the process of developing a portfolio.
3. A collaborative relationship can be developed between the teacher and administrator.
4. This type of portfolio development can be a precursor to developing a national board portfolio. (Hunter 1998)

Another reason teachers should develop a portfolio is to provide documentation about their professional life. Components of the portfolio also can be used to apply for teaching awards or leadership positions.

Organization

Teaching portfolios developed by teachers can have many different looks. However, there are two suggested ways for teachers to organize a professional portfolio for evaluation purposes and a different organization for other educators.

The first framework corresponds to the five standards from the National Board for Professional Teaching Standards (NBPTS). These can be combined into the categories of teaching, managing, and professional involvement. The advantage of this design is its simplicity. Since many teaching tasks are interrelated, the broadness of the first category allows teachers to include a variety of overlapping evidence. NBPTS standards for this category are: the teacher knows the subject he or she teaches, the teacher knows how to teach this subject, and the teacher is committed to students and their learning. The second category asks teachers to document their efforts in classroom management and student motivation. The NBPTS standard for this category is that teachers are responsible for managing and monitoring student learning. The third category, professional involvement, allows teachers to describe their professional involvement at the school, district, and national levels. The NBPTS standard is that teachers are members of learning communities.

The second suggested way to organize a portfolio is by professional goals. Many teachers often create a yearly professional development plan that contains one to three goals, and these goals often reflect school or district initiatives. The purpose of a professional goal portfolio is to promote self-learning, systematic reflection, and growth as professionals. These portfolios are similar to the product portfolio.

The organization of a professional goal portfolio is fairly simple:

1. State the professional goal.
2. Outline the goal and identify how it will be met.
3. Include evidence that shows how the goal was met.
4. Write a reflection on the goal.

One option for teachers who are constructing a professional goals portfolio is to develop a two- or three-year cycle. At the end of the first year, progress toward the goals is discussed. New goals that build on the original ones also may be added at this time. At the end of the cycle, the teacher evaluates his or her progress toward achiving those goals. For the next cycle, new goals are set.

Teachers who create portfolios as an alternative evaluation method learn many things about themselves. The authors' surveyed a variety of teachers who created portfolios and found two common responses to the process: "I like being in charge of myself," and "I could clearly see my own strengths and weaknesses based on evidence and the reflection process." In addition, many teachers who created portfolios on their own found the experience helpful when they later applied for National Board Certification.

Teaching Portfolios for Awards

Each year many teachers are awarded a "Teacher of the Year" award from their school, district, or state. Other awards are given by corporations or nonprofit organizations. Teachers who compete for these awards usually must compile portfolios. The purpose of an award portfolio is to show how award criteria are met. This is a showcase portfolio. Often, the format of these portfolios is set by the organization giving the award.

Teachers who are constructing showcase portfolios should pay particular attention to appearance. The first impression given by this portfolio can enhance a candidate's position. However, the depth of the portfolio's evidence and the teacher's reflections also is important and should not be neglected.

The showcase portfolio usually is divided into sections by the award criteria. Usually, a reflection is written for each section, though sometimes only one reflection is required for the entire portfolio. Clear labeling and headings are important in this portfolio because it will be reviewed by an external committee.

Teachers should make certain that the evidence they include and their reflections on that evidence support what is required for the award. It also is important for teachers to use their reflections to focus on the positive things happening in the classroom and to show how their activities led to student achievement.

Final Thoughts

Portfolio development gives teachers a chance to develop professionally. At any stage of a teacher's career, developing a portfolio can be an enlightening and enriching process. It can result in more effective teaching in the classroom and more focused teachers.

Being in charge of one's own professional development is a significant reason to consider portfolio development. Whatever the reason, portfolio development should be considered by every teaching professional.

Resources

Websites

www.nbpts.org

The website of the National Board for Professional Teaching Standards.

www.dpi.state.nc.us

Log on to find out more details on North Carolina's product portfolio model for continuing licensure.

http://curry.edschool.virginia.edu/curry/class/edlf/589_004/sample.html

Sample electronic portfolios created by preservice and inservice teachers.

http://www.uaa.alaska.edu/ed/tech/elport.html

Provides steps for developing an electronic portfolio and other sources for creating technology-based portfolios.

Books

Bird, T. "The Schoolteacher's Portfolio: An Essay on Possibilities." In *The New Handbook of Teacher Evaluation: Assessing Elementary and Secondary School Teachers*, edited by J. Millman and L. Darling-Hammond. Thousand Oaks, Calif.: Sage, 1990.

Bullock, A.A., and Hawk, P.P. *Developing a Teaching Portfolio: A Guide for Preservice and Practicing Teachers*. Columbus, Ohio: Prentice-Hall, 2000.

Cady, J. "Teaching Orientation: Teaching." *Education* 118, no. 3 (1998): 459-71.

Campbell, D.; Cignetti, P.B.; Melenyzer, B.J.; Nettles, D.H.; and Wyman, R.M., Jr. *How to Develop a Professional Portfolio: A Manual for Teachers*. California, Pa.: California University of Pennsylvania, 1997.

Hunter, A. "The Power, Production, and Promise of Portfolios for Novice and Seasoned Teachers." In *Professional Portfolio Models: Applications in Education*. Norwood, Mass.: Christopher-Gorden, 1998.

Interstate New Teacher Assessment and Support Consortium (INTASC). *Model Standards for Beginning Teacher Licensing and Development: A Resource for State Dialogue*. Washington, D.C.: Council of Chief State School Officers, 1992.

McLaughlin, M., and Vogt, M. "Portfolio Assessment for Inservice Teachers: A Collaborative Model." In *Professional Portfolio Models: Applications in Education*. Norwood, Mass.: Christopher Gordon, 1998.

Schon, D.A. *Educating the Reflective Practitioner*. San Francisco: Jossey-Bass, 1987.

Sparks-Langer, G.M., and Colton, A.B. "Synthesis of Research on Teachers' Reflective Thinking." *Educational Leadership* 48, no. 6 (1991): 37-44.

Articles

Holt, D.; Boulware, Z.; Bratina, T.; Johnson, A.C.; and Marquardt, F. "Integrating Preparation and Practice

Through a Technology-Based Approach to Portfolios for Professional Development Using CD-ROM Technology." *Resources in Education*. (1997). ERIC Document #ED 405 324.

James, A., and Cleaf, C. "Portfolios for Preservice Teachers." *Kappa Delta Pi Record* 30 (Winter 1990): 43-45.

King, B. "Thinking About Linking Portfolios with Assessment Center Exercises: Examples from the Teacher Assessment Project." Stanford: Teacher Assessment Project (TAP), Stanford University, 1990.

North Carolina Department of Public Instruction. "Performance-Based Licensure." http://www.dpi.state.nc.us. 2001.

Wolf, K. "The Schoolteacher's Portfolio: Issues in Design, Implementation, and Evaluation. *Phi Delta Kappan* 73 (October 1991): 129-36.

Recent Books Published by the Phi Delta Kappa Educational Foundation

100 Classic Books About Higher Education
C. Fincher, G. Keller, E.G. Bogue, and J. Thelin
Trade paperback. $29 (PDK members, $21.75)

Whose Values? Reflections of a New England Prep School Teacher
Barbara Bernache-Baker
Cloth. $49 (PDK members, $38)
Trade paperback. $24 (PDK members, $18)

American Education in the 21st Century
Dan H. Wishnietsky
Trade paperback. $22 (PDK members, $16.50)

Readings on Leadership in Education
From the Archives of Phi Delta Kappa International
Trade paperback. $22 (PDK members, $16.50)

Profiles of Leadership in Education
Mark F. Goldberg
Trade paperback. $22 (PDK members, $16.50)

**Use Order Form on Next Page
Or Phone 1-800-766-1156**

*A processing charge is added to all orders.
Prices are subject to change without notice.*

Complete online catalog at http://www.pdkintl.org

Order Form